RCODE
BREAKING THE SILENCE ON MALE ON MALE RAPE

Overcoming the Trauma and Confusion Left
After an Assault

JOHANNA SPARROW

RCode Revised Copyright © 2015-2017 Johanna Sparrow

All rights reserved.

Cover by: Mila

www.milagraphicartist.com

DEDICATION

To a wonderful soul, Elizabeth Iwona Flor.

Love and blessings always.

CONTENTS

Introduction

Men Don't Get Raped

The Attack

Loss of Manhood

Am I Gay?

Anger, Shame & Guilt

Who Can I Tell?

Lies I Tell Myself

Sexual Confusion

Letting Go

I am Okay

Recovery Zone

Listen to your Heart

ACKNOWLEDGMENTS

I would like to acknowledge the people in my life who have stood by my side no matter what has happened.

Introduction

Who would have ever thought male on male rape existed in this day and age? Not me! I was extremely shocked when I found out that male on male rape happens more often than we realize. My brothers were always taught by my father to be strong young men; to stand up for what is right and most of all, protect those around them because that is what men grow up to do. Nowhere in those father and son conversations were there ever talks of male on male rape.

Did you know that it is estimated that 10% of all sexual assaults are male on male rape? Male on male rape is said to be happening at an alarming rate and these acts are far from experimental.

The society looks down on male on male sexual assaults and it is this reason that it is rarely talked about in the society. Male survivors of rape try everything in their power to hide what has happened to them since there are very few aid programs with the focus on male on male rape or sexual assault. When sexual assaults are talked about, they are usually done so from a male on female, male on child or male on elderly perspective. Women and children seem to be the likely victims of such attacks and no other men. Why is this not part of a public campaign like those for women and children? Are men too strong to be seen as helpless when it comes to being raped by another male?

For many men, young men or boys who have suffered such attacks, I am sure the hurt and pain is unbearable. However, it may be nowhere close to the silence and secrecy they are forced to live with for the fear of what others would say about them. What I want you to know is that it was not your fault. Have you questioned your sexuality? Are you feeling confused about your sexuality? Do you feel broken or weak? All the questions are normal and you should know that this was something that was out of your control. Have you have turned to drinking or you are feeling helpless and now exhibit everything you were taught not to be? Do you see that what you are wrestling with is a psychological attack on your sexuality in your mind, since you did not defend yourself because you froze up at the time of the assault?

No matter what I have heard over the years, I have talked with many men who are now survivors, who still find it hard to face what has happened to them. A man of any size can be raped; most of my friends who were once victims are not small men. What they needed to hear was that no one has the right to abuse you. Also, no one has the right to do to you what has been done. You need to know that coming back from a sexual assault is not hard when you know it was not you who had the issues but your attacker.

For many men, the shame and humiliation following such an assault destroys them from within which in time reaches the core of their family if they are not helped in time.

"How do you tell your wife you were just raped by a friend after drinking?" This was the question one of the men I knew asked me with a devastating and broken expression on his face. I told him to tell his wife when he was ready and to know that what happened to him was not his fault.

When men become raped, they no longer trust any man and somehow blame themselves for not fighting back but freezing up instead. Many are emotionally disconnected because of the control and fear that is associated with such an attack. They fear they will be hated by their loved ones, friends, lovers and family if they ever find out. Worse, they feel responsible since they did not fight back or saying something to stop it. This is where sensitivity must take the place of one's anger and one must be able to understand that they are not to blame.

That no man wants to show vulnerability in their relationship is why many take being raped to their graves. I have seen some men shy away from all men and even have hatred to them where others are in constant need of approval from them.

I know many of my friends were never told that men get raped because as we know; a man can fight back and stop what women, the elderly and children can't do strength-wise However, since they were oblivious that they could be raped by their fellow men, a lot of damaged men have been taken advantage of by other men they felt they could trust. Rape on no level is okay or good but where is the voice of that man who has been the victim of adult rape by another man? For those who have suffered at the hands of others, know that you are not alone, and your voice that has been silent is now being heard no matter what you feel the society will think of you. The only way to stop this behavior is to acknowledge it once and for all because you are not crazy. Not being able to express yourself about what has happened to you leaves you trapped forever in a cycle of pain and mental abuse.

The healing process is real and can be achieved from a spiritual, physical and mental level, but it is going to have to start with you by letting go of all the fear and shame you have held on to for so long. I need you to believe me; this is not your fault! You did nothing to deserve this and you are still a man despite how you feel.

Men who rape other men are so tapped out of life's existence that they go around trying to conquer everything and everyone around them including other men. As long as you give what has happened to you power and fuel to control your life, it will not let go. Move out of that cell block into the freedom of knowing you are loved no matter what has happened to you. If I could see you right now, I would wrap my arms around you and tell you that you are loved, a man, and it was and could have never been your fault!

You will be surprised by how the love you receive will give you the strength to let go of that secret. You were a victim but today you are a voice for many who can't say or are afraid to say. You are a voice for many who are still going through it daily and live in a state of mental confusion. Most of all, you are a survivor!

The worse of what has happened to you is over now; it is time to advocate for others because you have a voice and the power to heal. If you don't know the signs of a male predator, hurt will help you find who is really in your company and around your family so that you can take control of the situation while overcoming the trauma and hurt focused on you by others.

Now if you are ready to confront your demons and move into the stages of healing to overcome what is happened to you, keep reading. Today you are not just a survivor; you are an overcomer!

CHAPTER ONE
SON, MEN DON'T GET RAPED

Whoever heard of a man getting raped? It just doesn't happen; I was told growing up with a house full of brothers. I had seen enough to know better as I got older; not just from close friends but within my family. The reality of someone close to me and I love dearly being attacked by another man brings tears to my eyes. I wanted to discuss how men become victims of rape and the only way to do so was to write until I could not write another word.

Let me first say to those I know that have experienced this horrific event that I have learned so much from you. I will also want you to know that by telling the world that men do indeed get raped by other men will shine light on why this happens. My hope is that this topic helps someone else who like many women out there feels men can't be victims of rape by their peers.

The truth is male on male rape is real! Did you know that male on male rape is one of the most under-reported crimes, and it happens to 1 out of 10 men? Did you know that male rape survivors are among the most under-served crime victims and till today, not much is being done to new victims daily? Instead of being protected by the society, many survivors find themselves battling the fact that they were sexually assaulted with the criminal justice system, social service providers, family, friends and their lovers who do not show support.

Rape can silence and even drive one to isolation and this is the case for survivors of male on male rape. They suffer enormous trauma that also causes their mind to take them to dark places that only a survivor or victim of rape or a sexual assault knows.

After someone else close to me broke his silence, it was like a flood gate of other men coming forward to tell their stories. These men were not gay nor did they think they were gay at the time of the attack. After the rape, they not only struggled with their identity but their sexuality as many were in relationships with women, married and struggling with addictions, divorce in a life of chaos.

Many of the survivors expressed being caught off-guard at the time it happened and that it was more than once. Not wanting to be insensitive to the unpleasant experience they had; I had to understand what would make someone to be around someone who has abused them in such a way. I realized it was not different from that of a woman trying to understand her attacker also known as Stockholm syndrome.

Is there such a thing in any case when someone is victimized that they lose their ability to protect themselves from what seemed like a dangerous and troubling situation? My dad has since passed away but somehow I am sure he knew male on male rape existed but he did not tell that to his sons.

Call it crazy, in wanting to protect those around you, but the truth is no one is safe when a predator's state of mind sends them out to get you. This has affected many around me and may have affected your life as well. Although resources that talk about this information don't expose it for all to see like other sexual assaults.

I can tell you as a woman that when I first embarked on this subject, I fought myself and did not want to deal with it. But like many subjects that touch home or within my circle, the devastation left behind by such an attack is heartbreaking. For this reason alone; I am moved to use my voice with the hope of discontinuing the ugly act.

Not many men will walk into a rape center to report their rape experience due to their concern of what will be thought of them after they leave. I have seen these men in a state of confusion and it is not their fault. For some, it happened when they were teenagers where they have been over powered by other domineering men. Others found themselves stuck in time over an event that caught them off-guard, following a night or day out with friends.

Many times, the man denies what has happened but it is their wrong way of thinking that put them in danger of another attack which studies have shown to have taken place. Depending on who is behind the assault, it can be subtle or aggressive, believe it or not. I am not talking about the ones doing the assault being gay because they might have wives and families like you which make them trustworthy to their friends.

Yet not every male on male sexual assault is wrapped in knowing the person, it could be someone you have just met. Men like this who walk the earth assaulting other men in a sexual way do so in secret, and may have had a history of sexual abuse growing up that was never dealt with in life. Their minds are messed up and they use that power to control others because of their own guilt, fear, hurt and pain.

It is a heartbreaking and heart wrenching tragedy that no one should have to live with fear. The shame is real like any sexual assault but what is clear here is that these men have been overpowered by their peers or someone they trusted. Many learn the signs and signals of what could be a dangerous situation due to that experience. I have been told by them how going out with friends no longer exist or getting to know other men is something they fear.

It may have happened with a co-worker, good friend or someone they thought was good to be around. What makes it hard to see for most men is that it is around things men do, like drinking, hanging out or watching sports just around guys. Below is a list of why men are told by their loved ones, fathers and mothers that men don't get raped:

o   They can stop any rape.

o   They are men and they are strong.

o   Men don't rape other men because they prefer women, children and the elderly; those they feel are weaker.

o   Men who rape men are both gay.

The truth is if someone wants to violate you, it doesn't matter who you are, they will do just that and it has nothing to do with size or gender. Men are raped daily, and not just in the prison cell but in their own homes by men they know and trusted at one time.

Still not enough information is given to men who find themselves in this position mainly because it is an embarrassment to talk about from a male perspective. Men of all walks of life are faced with this horrific secret that they keep to themselves because they are not gay and have families and lives that would not understand how such a thing could have happened to them.

This has to stop and more men must come forward to talk about what has happened to them but the fear of how they would be perceived by their family and friends is what keeps them in silence. Who wants to walk around worrying about how others see you when life is stressful enough? Some men would rather take this secret to their graves but it will cost them in their behaviors, actions and how they see themselves as time goes by if they do not seek help for what has happened to them.

The pain and hurt of being violated is the same no matter the gender. Just like other rape cases, the man ends up blaming himself for what took place. Taking the blame for someone who violates you will allow a male who has been raped to have some form of control over the events that took place. However, this way of thinking only adds confusion to an already confused situation.

Men who have been raped by their peers will question their sexuality or feel as if they may have wanted it in a strange way when that is just the mind's way of trying to understand what has happened to them. Don't buy into it!

What I feel about this is that inadequate education on rape is given to men in order for them to protect themselves because of the mindset that men have control over what happens to them. The truth be told; that is far from the truth. As I said earlier, anyone can become a victim at any time no matter their age, race or gender.

Below is a list of things men should tell their sons in the event that something like this happens.

o   Anyone can be a victim of rape at any time, a lot of evil and cruel people are in the world.

o   Being a man does not stop you from being raped; that is a myth.

o   There are many ways men get raped, and it is always unexpected by someone they knew or trusted.

o   Never be afraid to tell someone if you are a victim of rape.

o   Being a victim of rape does not change who and what you are.

o   Being a victim of rape can bring on a mixture of emotions from anger, rage, and shame to guilt. Those feelings normally result from what has happened.

o   You don't have to live in fear of being attacked again and can seek professional help.

o   Surround yourself with people who love you and don't doubt yourself or your sexuality.

o   Being raped by another man is not your Fault!

o   Being raped does not make you a gay.

o   Being raped does not make you weak or less of a person.

o   Being raped does not say you asked for it or did something to cause the attack.

o   Being raped does not make you less of a son, husband or father.

o   Being raped means you were a victim of someone's evil ways; no more no less.

o   That men get raped only in prison or jail is a myth.

Keeping an open mind about rape is the only way you can understand what has happened to you or someone you love. Size has nothing to do with rape since men who are tall and muscular still end up being raped. Understanding that rapists don't discriminate is the first line of defense against male on male rape.

CHAPTER TWO
THE ATTACK

Many men who are raped are caught off-guard when they are attacked. Maybe this was the case for you and still till this day, you live with that secret. How long ago were you attacked? Did you tell someone you trusted? Do you walk around angry? I can tell you that your feelings, although extreme, are real and maybe something that you may not want to face.

Are you married with kids or in a serious relationship with a woman and now your world has been turned upside down or have you been battling with the fact that you were raped for days, months or years? Were you drinking when the attack happened? Do you remember everything that happened to you? I am sure this was the most frightening thing you had to experience, being violated. You are hurt and the pain is real, so don't try to doubt that. You were not dreaming. What happened to you was wrong and most of all, it wasn't your fault!

Rape Stories

John, aged 23, had been working late at his new job and went with Phil, his boss, to the pub for a drink. Because he lived a long way from where he worked, John took up Phil's offer to stay at his home for the night. Back at his place, Phil went to kiss John. When John pushed him away, Phil got angry and hit him. John was scared he would be really hurt or killed. He froze and could do nothing to protect himself as Phil proceeded to sexually assault him. John hasn't told any of his friends and family why he quit his job. He has discovered he was becoming more and more depressed as the weeks go by. He feels ashamed that he did not fight off his attacker.

Dean, aged 34, was at a party with his girlfriend. She took the car home early because she was working the next day. Because he was feeling too drunk to walk, Dean accepted a lift home from a guy he had met at the party. On the way home, the man stopped his van, pulled Dean into the back and raped him. Dean is 190cm tall and weighs 85kg.

Mark was walking home from a football game through a park near his home. Two men grabbed him from behind. While one held him down, the other raped him. For two months afterwards, Mark had very frightening flashbacks of the assault. During these flashbacks, he felt as though it was happening all over again. He still feels ashamed that he got an erection while the assault was taking place, even though his counselor had told him that this was not at all uncommon.

Lee was 17 when his older brother forced him to have oral sex in the shower one day. His brother told him not to bother telling anyone because they wouldn't believe him. Because boys had often called him a poofter at his school and because his brother was engaged to be married, Lee thought what his brother said was true.

Jason had gone out to a party with some friends. While he was there, he met two guys who asked him back to their place for coffee later. When they arrived, they had a joint and some more to drink. Jason thought the drink tasted a bit strange at first but then thought no more about it. Jason woke up in a strange bed the next day with no recollection of what had happened during the night. He was aware, however, that his anus was very sore. He got out of the house as quickly as he could. Jason went to a sexual health clinic for an STD screening but did not tell the doctor what had happened. Six months later, he knows he has not contracted any sexually transmitted diseases but the discomfort and lack of trust he feels around men is still causing him problems.

I have spoken to a few men who have come out and told me they were raped or a victim of a rape in a roundabout way. At the end of the day, this does not make you less than a man. I remembered being told by a good friend of mine how they were attacked. Although I was stunned to hear that, much of how that person felt was no different from any other rape victim I have spoken with over the years.

I will call this person Jones when telling his story. I must say that

that evening, I was not expecting to hear such detail on how he was victimized by someone he knew. In his own words he started to share how upon having this person over one evening to watch a college basketball game things went wrong. He explained that after a few drinks; something they did many times while watching the game, this so called friend pulled out a knife and told him to strip down. He hesitated at first when he thought his assumed friend was playing around but taken that the knife was real and this person's expression was scary, he succumbed fearfully and did what was asked of him eventually.

Not sure what was going on, he thought his friend was clowning around on "some gay shit" as he put it until his friend told him to lay face down on the floor, but not before taking off his boxers. He remembers begging his friend to put the knife away and to stop playing around although he was fearful for his life.

He followed everything his friend asked of him in shock and remembered how painful it was when his friend penetrated him. He also remembered his face being pushed into the carpet while his friend held him down and sodomized him. He begged for his friend to please stop but by that time, it was too late and he had been raped in a blink of an eye.

He remembered closing his eyes with his mouth open while his friend took advantage of him, and had never told a soul until now. His friend rushed around putting on his clothes while he laid there. When his friend left his house, he remembered slowly getting up because he was in so much pain and taking a shower before his wife got home.

He said he was dazed and felt vulnerable from that moment on around other men. He never spoke to that friend again after the attack and never told anyone what happened. To this day, he still walks around with that shame of what took place eight years ago. He still is full of hurt and pain from what happened to him.

Talking to him, I could see the hurt and pain in his eyes as his voice cracked when he recounted each and every event that took place that night. Is he alright now? The answer would be no, he is still working on finding that place he was in before the rape took place. He expressed how he only thought such things happened to men in prison or in jail. The funny thing is that the friend is married and was married when this happened. I am sure neither of them told their family members.

Upon talking to another man who was raped, he recounted how his attack was from his boss while out of town for business. In his memory about what happened, his boss made a proposition towards him after drinks in the lobby of the hotel which he did not say anything other than ending the night early. His boss later showed up as his hotel room door, wanting to come in to apologize; claiming it was the drinks and that he wasn't him in his right frame of mind.

Well as you would guess, he let his manager in his hotel room only for the worse to happen. His boss forced himself on him. According to him, he froze! He did not fight back and he mentioned the unbearable pain he felt while being raped. When his boss was done, he left him in an unimaginable position. He claimed he laid there for the rest of the night unable to move or get up. He was not able to talk to his wife that night for fear of what she would think of him if he told her. He felt alone, ashamed and angry.

The following morning, he remembered meeting his boss in the lobby while his boss acted as if nothing had happened while he was still in pain as well as shock. When the business trip was over, he remembered not being able to go to work and at that moment, he quit his job. He could not face his boss or worse, he was fearful of what his boss might do to him if he said something. For years he has tried to wrap his mind around what happened to him and couldn't stop asking "why him?".

Was his boss gay or even worse; was he gay and did not know it? Because of this he is in a state of confusion, he lost his family and turned to alcohol to keep him from losing his mind. He is a struggling alcoholic and battles this evil that was done to him alone. He has been in and out of jail for drunk driving due to not being able to get over what happened to him.

Becoming a victim of rape can happen anywhere and at any time especially when alcohol is involved. It does not matter if you are on a business trip or you are just hanging out with friends. As you can see, the story is almost the same in that they were drinking and someone they never expected such molestation from molested them. Most men who are raped and are unable to report for fear of what their loved ones would keep it to themselves and have it manifest later on in them as bad habits or addictions.

"I thought you could get raped in jail only and not in the comfort of your own home or the home of someone that you have known for a long time." This is what many male victims of rape say, which leads them to a more sensitive side of themselves as well as the needs of other rape victims. Why is it so difficult to walk away from being a victim of rape if you are a man? How can you get past how you feel deep inside? Have you cried about what has happened to you? Are you living your life based on who you were before the rape but can't seem to get a grip on your manhood because you feel it was taken from you and you did nothing to stop it? Does that make you gay? Let me tell you that it does not make you gay and most importantly; you don't have to keep reliving your attack if you understand that it was not your fault.

Many rape victims place blame it on themselves as if it is going to make those feelings go away and bring you back to the person you were before it happened, it will not!

The pain you felt during the attack can leave you hurting and in pain for the rest of your life if you don't get a hold of what is going on. Your mind is trying to make sense of what happened and your response to what took place. I have learned that in horrific events like this, your mind can work in your healing or in your demise especially if you think a certain way about your manhood.

You may be living with this nightmare and have lost your family and friends because they don't understand what is happening to you. This is the worst thing that can be done to a man; it can ruin his life and his mind. Survivors of male on male rape do find healing. Even if they don't have all the answers to their disturbing questions, they learn to accept what has happened to them and move on. You have the control to take back your life and find peace within your heart. You can let go of what happened to you no matter how long ago you have held onto it. Many of you are devastated within because of such an attack or even questioned who and what you are since you no longer know.

This normal type of weirdness is understandable for what you have gone through but you can't carry this secret alone nor for the rest of your life. Hasn't it cost you enough? Why continue to feed it the control of your fear or lack of control over your life today? This is not to say that you have to pull it together since I am sure you may have had that talk with yourself a thousand of times, but you have to wake up now. Wake up and start living again knowing that a rape does not make you nor does it take away your value as a person. Walking around dazed years later does not make you crazy, gay or make it your fault. You are still a man, son, brother, husband and dad, you just have to tell yourself that.

Yes, you were a victim of an attack and now you are a survivor. It is understood that men in prison or jail are raped. But it happened to you and it was not something you asked for; just like women don't ask to be raped. The sad truth about what you went through is that the person that betrayed your trust and violated you may have been plotting that for a long time even if they gave no signals they were gay.

When a man rapes you, it is about control that that person wants to have over you for whatever sick reason. Many times, these attacks come through hanging out and a few drinks. Did you know that it happens more than you know and many of the people in your circle may have gone through the same thing. They are just not able to talk about it and they live in a silent world alone. Below is a list of symptoms you will have when trying to deal with being raped by another man.

o   Disbelief

o   Fear

o   Anger and Shame

o   Insomnia

o   Night terrors

o   Lack of trust around other men

o   Questioning your sexuality

o   Faulting yourself for what happened or not being able to stop it

o   Guilt

o   Embarrassment

o   Addictions

o   Drug abuse

o   Alcohol abuse

o   Not being able to have a healthy relationship

o   Feeling as if you lost your manhood

o   Loss of appetite

o   Weight loss or weight gain

o   Depression

o   Suicidal thoughts

o   Rage

o   Confusion

o   Anxiety

These stages of hurt and pain can be in any order. The constant feeling of being dirty is another feeling you will experience but know that this too is what to expect when you are dealing with a rape. Stop beating yourself up over what you should and could have done because this is not going to aid you in the healing process. The only person that is looking down on you is yourself and today is the day that you must find healing even if that is telling someone you love and trust.

You no longer need to carry this secret alone. Allow someone you love to help you carry this pain and hurt. In doing this, you will see how you will begin to let go of your past although you will never forget. Below is a list of ways to start the healing process no matter how long ago the rape was.

o   Tell someone so that they can help you.

o   Tell yourself every day that you are a man and that rape does not take away from that.

o   Be open for change and cry if you have too.

- Knowing that you are facing your rape head on rather than in your mind is not going to make you a victim again.

- When getting to know others, keep alcohol out of the process.

- Know that a rape does not make you gay no matter how confusing you are now that it has happened.

- Forgive yourself for not fighting back or stopping what happened to you.

- Stop blaming yourself for the acts of another.

- Stop questioning your sexuality and manhood, they have nothing to do with being violated.

- Talk to a professional in the field if you don't trust those around you or you should read books that will help you deal with overcoming rape.

Know that you are not the first and will not be the last man on earth to become a victim of rape by another man. Also know that rape is real, and it does not just happen in a prison cell or jail cell as society will have you to believe, it happens everywhere. Most of all, know that you can overcome everything that you are feeling no matter how long you have been feeling this way. You can't live life looking back no matter how bad it was!

CHAPTER THREE
LOSS OF MANHOOD

So you were raped and for some time now you have been living life around those you love as if nothing has happened to you. The worst part of that day or night is that your manhood was stripped away from you in seconds and not only did this person sodomize you, but they did so to your heart and mind. You are a walking time bomb full of hate and anger. Although you pray, you can't find the peace you need to make the pain of it all go away.

You would give anything to make the flashbacks stop; including taking your own life. You are lost within and for the sake of your soul, you don't know who you are each passing day. Why did they do this? You question yourself everyday as if you will ever know the answer, you won't. What you need to know is that rape has more to do with control and nothing else. Controlling you was what this person wanted to do.

Did they really take your manhood or is it in your mind that you have come to think this way? What determines manhood anyway? Are you still all who you are and much more? Are you living your life as a victim and finding issues with every man you meet because you don't and can't trust them? I am sure the guy did not walk around with rapist on his forehead or you would not be in this position, right? No he did not nor do you have gay or loss of manhood stamped across your forehead. I know from all outer appearances that you are a hundred percent man, but your mind and heart tell you differently. Even worse; a certain part of your body has experienced trauma.

Right now, you may be feeling as if no one understands you or what you have been through but trust me when I tell you that rape no matter who the rapist is, never is an easy pill to swallow. If you have found yourself in a confused state because of rape and now you don't know where you stand when it comes to your preference to date a male or female, know that this confused state is not normal. However, as a result of what you have gone through, it makes perfect sense.

Your life has been altered; that is no doubt and you feel it in everything you do. The worst part is that you feel as if you can't go to your dad because of his strong belief that men don't get raped; what would he think of you? You not only carry around your own hurt, pain and shame but that of what your family members would think of you. I tell you that it is a lot of weight to carry around.

Below are lists of symptoms one may feel after being raped by another man.

o   They are not sure if they like the opposite sex or not.

o   Not sure if they enjoyed what happened to them or not.

o   They ejaculated at the time of the rape which sends a mixed message that they may have enjoyed it.

o   They are now attracted to men instead of women.

o   Notice the attention that they get from men.

o   Have multiple partners of the opposite sex

o   Unable to take back control of their life.

Although they are a few above that I have mentioned, I am more than sure that there are many more feelings or symptoms a man who has been raped by another man feels. It is as if a switch was turned on in your head and the perception you have of yourself and those around you is life changing. Are you comfortable being around other men? Do you struggle with having an attraction to them? Are you resentful or angry and hate being around any man? If so, you are not alone and many men who have been raped express the same exact feelings that you are having at this moment, but still, they refuse to seek help or talk to someone who can help them understand their feelings.

Some men find themselves in unhealthy relationships with women and feel the only way to get their manhood back is by having multiple partners of the opposite sex. They can't or no longer have a desire to settle down with one woman and one can find them all over the place in an unhealthy state of mind.

Below is a list of things you can do to help gain control back over your life.

o   Stop sleeping around in an effort to find your manhood. I can tell you it is not in anyone's bed.

o   Learn what a true man is and how he handles life traumas and match your actions up to what has happened to you.

o   Get your mind right and know that a violation does not equal a loss of who and what you are.

o   Stop blaming yourself for what you should have done and accept yourself no matter what has happened to you.

o   Know that this person who has done this to you had motives long ago when they entered into your life and that was to violate you.

o   Stop giving your rapist power over you through sex.

o   Know that you are a man and will forever be a man until you leave this world.

o   Find forgiveness within yourself for the things you have no control over no matter what others may think.

Stop caring about what others will think of you. If they love you, then the only thing you should feel is their love and support.

Know that you are going to feel out of sorts and you will have good days as well as bad days; it is alright. You are still a work in progress and your mind and feelings will have you in and out at times; never feeling connected or complete. Give it time and trust that you will get past those emotions that you find yourself struggling with daily. If you are not finding yourself crawled up into a tight ball crying but rather feeling as if you no longer belong here, I would rather you cry it out and leave all thoughts of not feeling life outside on the curb. This means when you leave, don't pick it up and bring it inside with you.

Bad things happen every day to good people but you still must go on and live life. Your failure to do so only empowers your rapist. If you feel as if you want to report your rape to the police by all means, do so. This person needs to be stopped. Many men who are the victims of a rape never ever tell the police because of what they would look like.

You have a voice and that voice should never be silent for no reason at all. If you ever wanted to scream but, like so many victims of rape or sexual assault, felt that you could not at the time of the attack, now is your time to scream. You need to scream now to let out all the trapped negative energy you were unable to release due to not wanting to show weakness

CHAPTER FOUR
AM I GAY?

Since you had the rape incident, you have been left in a state of depression followed by sexual confusion, and don't know how to feel. You have been mentally and emotionally traumatized by the attack and no one around you seems to understand or know what to do to help you.

You find that you have been wearing your feeling on both sides of your shoulders and cry or get depressed at a drop of a hat. One minute you are okay with everything and the next minute you hate the skin that you are in. You find yourself dropping your head or even sticking out your chest when men look you in the face. Either way, you have something to say but not sure what that is at this time.

Ever since the attack, you shy away from sex and find that you are not able to perform like you once did. Is your sex life over? Have you turned gay since the attack? Why can't you seem to get it together? Can other men tell you were raped or worse gay? No, you are not gay, and looking at someone who may be shy or drop their head does not say anything about the type of person you are.

You can't tell if someone has been raped by how they act unless they tell you that they were and the same is true for a rapist. It is not how a person looks that makes them a predator or victim but what they say. Many times, you can see it in their behavior or in the things they may say. However, that is if you feel something which many people don't or if they do, they block those feelings or brush them off as if it is their mind playing games on them.

If you are no longer dating the opposite sex, that is you and nothing else. Maybe you need more time to heal and nothing is wrong with that; you should take all the time that you need. Never let anyone tell you that you should be over a traumatic event such as a rape. Many times, insensitive people can say things that are really messed up; don't be intimidated or abused by anyone. Below is a list of things you can do to help you get over the confused state you now find yourself battling:

o   Process what has happened to you and know that it is okay to feel sad or even cry.

o   Scream out if you have to. Many rape victims out of fear hold back their emotions but you must release your emotions to have your peace of mind.

o   Don't force yourself to go out with anyone . Giving yourself time to understand you have been violated and a part of you is in pain is okay.

o   The pain that you experience and still feel today is real. Don't doubt yourself or blame yourself for not knowing this would happen.

Did you know that thinking one is gay after such an attack is what many men who are victims of rape deal with daily? You are not alone. Right now, sex should be the last thing on your mind so that you can really deal with everything. This is the same process many women go through after such an attack. They keep wondering if they asked for it or if they had done something to cause it.

Many female victims of rape find themselves going from man to man as if this is the only way they have some sort of control or peace of mind about what is going on. Feeling guilty is common after a sexual assault; you found that you are feeling guilty about a lot of things. If you were in a relationship when you were attacked, you and the person that attacked you know that you will find yourself lost in a mixture of emotions. Nevertheless, you must keep in mind that your silence about what has happened can add to that confusion.

This does not mean that you have to go out and speak out against male on male rape. You just need to find healing for yourself.

I have talked to many men who find it hard to get past their attack because they are still in contact with the man that raped them no matter how crazy that is. For many men, being able to get back to the relationship you once had with the person before the rape is better than dealing with things on their own. This brings about confusion and anger.

Many men who keep in contact with the man that raped them find it easy when both place blame on alcohol or some type of drug which makes it easy to dismiss. Know that you are more than the rape you went through and that your manhood is intact. Sure, things may seem and feel out of sync compared to what you were used to feeling but know that you went through something that is not the norm, even though it happens every day.

Being raped by another man does not make you gay; not at all. You have to understand that men who are gay are gay by choice. So, where is the choice in rape? Did you have a say in what happened to you? Were you thinking this way before the rape? Did you see yourself as a healthy heterosexual male before the rape? If your answers are you were not thinking this way and only desired women. Then, you must know that the answer to the question of you being gay is, you are not. Maybe you liked the feeling you got at the time of the attack, which is what may be confusing to you.

You need to know that your body was forced into stimulation and nothing else. This happens to women who are raped as well when they climax during the attack, but does that mean they wished to be raped? No! The body when tampered with in that area will and can be stimulated out of fear, not that you wanted it or it felt good.

What if I told you that it meant nothing just because you ejaculated? Below is a list of reasons one will ejaculate during a rape:

o   Fear

o   Confusion

o   Shock

o   Stimulation

This has nothing to do with if you were willing or not. Now does that make sense to you? Have you confronted the person who has done this to you and are you still communicating with him? If so, the first thing you must do is cut off all contact and move on with your life.

If this person has threatened you in the past that if you say something, he would hurt you or those you love, don't let that stop you from living or telling someone.

Know that you will be looked at as a liar by some people but not everyone. People have different thoughts about who they feel are victims. They may feel you wanted it or could have stopped it but don't listen to them. If you are a father, the best thing you can do is to educate young men about sexual assaults that men can be a victim of rape, just as women or children.

I have seen lives change for the worse or the better after rape with men and women, even though it is a daily struggle. You must know that you are strong and one day of a horrible event does not change that. You also must know that you are loved, and trust those around you who have proven their love and loyalty to you.

When was the last time you looked at yourself in the mirror? Did you really look or turn away? Did you like what you saw or were you disappointed? You will not feel this way for long, now that you are really dealing with your emotions and feelings. You were born a man and you are a man no matter what happens to you outside of your control. You and only you can decide who and what you are. Only you can decide that you are not a victim.

Don't be tricked into thinking you are something that you are not. if anything, you were violated and victimized. To be honest with you; neither one of those makes you gay. When you begin to challenge your mind and what it is telling you is when you will begin to heal. Below are keys words you can use to start to train your mind after a sexual assault has left you confused.

- I am a man.

- I did not ask for this rape nor is it my fault.

- I was not thinking about having sex when I was raped.

- I am still a heterosexual male.

- I still see the beauty in women and don't need to sleep with them all to find my manhood.

o   I have nothing against gay men, I am just not one of them.

o   Someone forced their belief on me and that does not make their belief my belief.

Now can you feel a change taking place in your mind? There is power in words especially truth. Never allow someone's idea of you or their beliefs force you to be confused about who you are and what you are. I have been around many men who have been the victims of rape by other men and don't see themselves the same way. I have had people close to me tell me, "I never thought I would be a victim." This is one of the many reasons why I felt it was important to shine light on this horrible act when it happens to a man. The world must know that you suffer no different from any rape victim; the only difference is that more of you suffer in silence.

CHAPTER FIVE
ANGER, SHAME & GUILT

Men who become the victims of rape never see it coming and will tell you so if you ever have the chance to sit down and talk to them. They are in shock, never thinking in a million years they would become the victim of rape by another man. Men are not only raped by men but they can become the victim by the hands of a woman. The trauma is still real and that reality of hurt and pain cannot be measured no matter how much you try. Are men who are raped by other men angry as some would have you believe? Yes, no one looks to be assaulted no matter the gender.

Men are easy victims just as women are too. This is because they are not aware of every man's motives. Not every night of social drinking is innocent. In fact, many men who rape use this tactic more easily on men because most men are seen in settings where alcohol is involved. A night of social drinking has cost many men to become victims of rape, a shame they carry to this day.

How do you explain having sex with another man when you are said to be heterosexual with a girlfriend or wife and kids at home? Sadly, this is not a topic a victim easily goes to talk about. When it happens to a man, he is more likely to fall into a state of confusion about his sexual identity.

The anger a male victim of rape experiences is a mixture of many feelings with one being unable to stop the rape or not being able to remember what happened to them but waking up with a horrible anus pain. Remembering or not remembering what happened to them is what brings about the anger and shame.

The stages that a male rape victim goes through are no different from the many stages that all rape victims go through irrespective of their gender. Their pain and hurt is real, and the shame of not being able to stop it or worst, trusting someone who attacked them in a weakened state is a mixture of hurtful feelings they walk around with daily.

Guilt plays a serious role in the mind of the rape victim, and it is this feeling they are unable to get past or let go. If you have ever had to live through this, you know that it is a nightmare and worse; you are not able to find a way out. How long have you held this secret? Do you feel there was more you could have done to stop it or worse, should you have known the person you had in your friends circle was thinking this way? Are they still in your life acting as if nothing happened? If this is the case, you have located some of your anger but this by far is not all of it. Below is a list of ways you feel after a sexual assault.

o   Anger

o   Shame

o   Disbelief

o   Embarrassment

o   Rage

o   Insomnia

o   Loss of appetite

- o   Increase appetite

- o   Fear of other men

- o   Guilt

- o   Thoughts of hurting your attacker

- o   Helplessness

As you can see, each feeling carries its own weight and timeframe of getting out of that state of mind. I have had men who have been raped ask me if they would ever find themselves again. My answers are always the same; "You will be better than you were." This may not be the answer many male raped victims want to hear but it is an honest one since it is not where you are today but where you see yourself.

At this moment, I am sure you have been in a lot of pain and confusion over what has happened to you. Understand that your feelings are validated and you should never feel ashamed or hang your head in embarrassment since you did not do anything, it was all done to you and that is a fact. I know you are much more aware of your surroundings today then you have ever been as well as who you allow in your inner circle. The truth is you have every right to be this way.

The only thing I ask is that you don't allow what has happened to you consume your life and take away from it since it was not your fault. If you are struggling in your anger, shame and guilt to hold on to your family or relationships, know that this is the stage where you have to work hard. Don't submit yourself to the tricks the mind can play on you like having you to walk away from those people in your life that you love or worse, take out your anger and rage on the wrong people.

If you are feeling as if you are holding on emotionally by the tips of your fingers like holding onto a ledge, scared of falling, you have to trust yourself and pull yourself up to a place where you can cope until you find that place from within where you can exist. Below are lists of things you can do to stop fighting out at the ones you love.

- Find new people you can trust.

- Clean house and get rid of those people in your life who may still be in touch with the person who raped you.

- Manage your anger, shame and guilt by knowing where those feelings come from, not your fault.

- If you don't like the word "victim", choose another word that you feel comfortable with that describes what you went through.

- Love yourself daily.

- Take up a new sport or hobby to get your mind off what has happened to you.

- It is never too late to file a police report and know that you still can do that if you want.

- Ending your connection with the person who has hurt you and any connections with those who still have that person in their life.

- Find new places to go out and if you drink, keep alcohol out of your life if you can.

Cleaning up your life and getting back on track is not hard or easy but you must follow a few steps so that you don't take out what it is you are dealing with on those around you. Don't allow rape to destroy your life. I have said this to a few good friends of the family who still to this day cannot get what happened to them out of their heads and don't look at their manhood. I told them they still have a good way to go.

I remember one day my husband and I met up with some old friends for dinner. We spent time with them since we had not seen each other for what felt like months due to all of our schedules. We must have laughed and discussed everything under the sun as if we were never going to see each other again Then suddenly, the topic took a turn towards something more serious; rape in jail.

Not sure why we were talking about this; my husband and I went with the flow of things because as much as it was a topic out of left field, it was an interesting one in that male on male rape in prison is out of control. The question was even asked if it would still be considered rape taken you are already locked up. It could even be worse for many men in jail faced with their manhood being taken. One cannot but ask, "Could this also be more of an additional punishment?"

Either way, I was all but ready to talk about issues and when I conveniently posed the question of male on male rape outside of prison, and the number of men who don't come forward, you could feel the energy in the room change.

Our friend Joe, I will call him, suddenly dropped his head as if I said something wrong, but did I? It was clear something was on his mind and not sure what it was. We all waited for him to say what was on his mind. Clearly by his response, he must have known someone who experienced this, I assumed. But I was shocked when he slowly brought into focus a situation that happened several years ago and how he had an encounter with another man. He asked if that made him gay. Apparently this has been the number one discussion in his home with his current wife who is as pretty opened-minded as him when it comes to topics like this.

But wait, was I hearing my good friend right? He had a sexual encounter with another man or was I reading too much into what he was saying? So I waited for him to tell his story and listened with open ears.

As he recounted every detail in his head, I could see he was not comfortable telling us his story but the more I listened, the more I realized that he was raped. He did not consent to anything. As he told it, he had given a friend who was having car issues a ride home. They decided to hang out the rest of the evening which as he explained was no big deal because his wife was out of town on business and he really did not have much to do anyways other than sit around in his house alone.

The guy's car was placed in a shop and would be ready the following day so they both decided to make it a guy's night and have his friend stay over since it was easy for him to take him to get his car in the morning. Furthermore, he lived a good distance away and he was not up for the drive. He made them a few drinks, and he ordered something in since he was no cook and they both sat and watched an old baseball game he taped earlier.

He remembered going to bed only to be awakened by what he described as a heavy pressure on his back, it was the guy climbing on top of him. He remembered asking him what the heck he was doing and why he was in his room. Drunk, the guy pushed over onto his side and told him not to say a word. He said at first, he was trying to get his drunk friend off him and out of his house but the guy who was two times his size used his strength and weight against him, pinning him down to have sex with him.

The sad part, he remembered having a mixture of emotions; some good and some bad but more on the humiliating side and felt pain when he sat down, something he could not explain. The guy left his home, and he never saw him again which he explained caused him to go in and out about his feelings and emotions.

More so, he knew he was to blame since he knew the guy was bisexual and causally flirted with him from time to time but he did nothing about and it and saw it as harmless. For a while, he felt he too must be bisexual in that he never put the guy in place for flirting with him so it was as if he asked for it.

He gave mixed messages and may have confused the guy because he was confused about his sexuality off and on through the years; just he never acted out those thoughts. I told Joe that he was raped and his own confusion had nothing to do with it. He was married to a woman and had never acted on his thoughts. Seeing a few men as cute is not going to put you in the gay category, I said. The truth is I told him if this guy had been flirting with him, he was interested in him and he took things too far. Rape does not mean you said yes which would explain why he was on his third marriage.

Seeing our friend in this condition was heartbreaking since I know the hurt and pain a rape can leave one in. After telling him that he was raped, and it was not his fault nor did he consent to what happened to him, he kind of nodded his head back and forward a few times then excused himself for fresh air. My husband went out after him while I sat with his wife. As you can guess, the rest of the night was pretty heavy since none of us was expecting to hear that, but I guess Joe could no longer live with the confusion of what took place, I understood he needed answers.

Could this have been the fuel behind his anger and not feeling understood in his last two marriages? How long was he dealing with this? What is understood is that the secret he planned to keep to himself became bigger than he expected and could no longer carry it alone, I am happy my husband along with his wife was there for him.

Today he is taking things one day at a time and has decided to see it for what it was, rape and nothing else, although at times, he feels helpless because of it but he is working to get his mind and heart right. No one should have to live with being a victim of anything. If you have people around you who love you and you feel you are ready to share your story, do so since a strong support team can help you get back to where you want to be.

CHAPTER SIX
WHO CAN I TELL?

When a man is raped, they struggle with telling what has happened to them just like any rape victim but for them, it has more to do with the fact that men don't get raped and especially not by other men. Like many victims of rape, men have a hard time finding someone to trust and tell what has happened to them. They cry in silence!

Men who are victims of rape don't seek out people to tell their stories too because they don't want to be looked at as being gay or worst, not being believed. For the many male on male victims of rape walking around today, they don't know what is worse saying that they were the victim of rape and some man held them down and took their manhood or to hear that they are lying and may be gay.

When a woman is raped, she has to live with not being believed and that she wanted it and not being called anything else. Men who suffered the attack of another man walk around not sure of what to do and how to act. Something is missing. It is as if they have lost parts of themselves during and after the attack and now live in a mental torment. Most men cover up what has happened to them by bed hopping while never committing to anyone or trusting their heart.

Below are lists of things men who have become victims of rape suffer through from day to day.

o Doubt

o Confusion

o Fear of someone finding out

o Sexual confusion about one's identity

o Insomnia

- Anger
- Aggression
- Guilt
- Grief
- Suicidal thoughts
- Regret
- Low-self esteem
- Shame and depression
- Loss of control
- Trust Issues
- Helplessness

The list can go on and on in terms of how one will feel following a sexual attack. The truth is many male victims of rape hide themselves away from others in an effort to protect themselves.

Some victims even become sensitive to certain comments or phrases which alter their relationship with others. Why are so many men suffering in silence? Why is it that being a rape victim not only steals the victim's life but their identity? Why is the silence when it comes to male on male rape so guarded? All the feelings that a man goes through after a rape is that crazy kind of normal for what he is dealing with!

Many men who are victimized by others can see their way out of their pain and find themselves cycling back daily to the events and acts of the rape. What may be hidden to others is a constant image in the mind of the victim. For the many men who have gotten past the victim stage, they never see themselves the same and would avoid any situation that puts them in a vulnerable state or a stage of a victim. If they are not attacking everything someone is saying, they are living their life on the edge because they are yet to stop the images or the feelings of helplessness they felt at the time of the attack.

Who can a male victim of rape talk to when they are ready to stop the hurt and pain they constantly feel? It can be a pastor, loved one or counselor.

Below is a list of places someone can reach out to when they have been the victim of a rape or sexual assault:

Rainn, Rape Abuse & Incest National Network at 1-800-656-4673

https://www.rainn.org/

Joyful Heart Foundation, 1 in 6 Partnership and 1 Blue String; Supporting Male Survivors

http://www.joyfulheartfoundation.org/programs/education-awareness/engaging-men/1in6-partnership-and-1bluestring?gclid=CKSVhMOr5MUCFcQkgQodBr4APQ

To locate a rape crisis center in your area, you can search the internet.

National Suicide Prevention Lifeline at 1-800-273-8255

http://www.suicidepreventionlifeline.org/

For Depression you can visit, Your Life Your Voice at 1-800-448-

3000

http://www.yourlifeyourvoice.org/Pages/home.aspx

24 hours prayer hotline, Trinity Broadcasting Network (TBN) 1-877-731-1000. For those who seek spiritual counsel.

http://www.tbn.org/contact/

If nothing more; I seek to provide advice, information and reassurance to men who have been raped. I encourage you to seek help or counseling from a specialist who understands what you are going through to help you overcome the trauma you are experiencing. Still that is not enough, I know, and you have to deal with family, friends and lovers who may not have a clue on how to understand you when you are not yourself.

If you are the loved one of a victim of rape, the best thing that you can do is learn to be understanding and give it time. You may not know what to believe or may have been given a variety of stories by the victim as a way to cope, they need time. Some men even change their appearance and or career in order for them to live or come close to some form of a normal life as before. Below is a list of negative ways a victim of rape can handle what has happened to them:

o   Turning to Alcohol.

o   Turning to drugs.

o   Turning to people who are destructive.

o   Turning their back on family and friends.

o   Leaving their job or stop working.

o   Walk around in fear and shame.

o   Become confrontational with other males as a way to gain control.

o   Seek out male validation.

o   Become controlling.

o   Developmental issues or disorders.

You may have been raped and suffer with the ability to cope in what one would call a normal world but know that you must learn how to deal with each and every emotion one at a time. What happened to you was horrific and wrong and you have a right to be upset and angry. Nevertheless, don't let that anger keep you from living life and loving the people who are there to support you.

As long as you know that everything you are feeling is okay and you are not the one at fault for what has happened to you, then you are well on your way to healing. In order for healing to take place, you must be willing and ready to let go of what has happened to you no matter how many times it happened. You owe no one an explanation. Below are how you start the healing process from the inside out:

o   Forgiveness.

o   Knowing it was not your fault.

- You don't have to live life as a victim.

- Trusting yourself.

- Stop seeking validation from other men.

- Know that you are safe.

- Open up and share your story with people you trust and love.

- Stop walking around in guilt and shame.

- Know that peace comes from within and even though something was taken from you by the rapist, what they did not take was your life or soul and that you are safe.

There will be times where you will feel as if each and every step is hard to deal with but know that as long as you do what you have to do, you will be okay. Don't worry about the process of letting go, your heart and mind will eventually do that for you. Therefore, you have to be willing to let it happen since many male rape victims want to hold on to what has happened to them as a way to protect themselves. The truth is all it really does is keep them scared, angry and victimizing themselves.

When you let go, you gain something in its place and that is strength. Are you living as a trapped victim in your mind? Do you hate life? You are not alone since many men who do talk about being raped feel this way. Their ability to trust or socialize with other men becomes non-existing, and that is okay since you have to do what makes you feel safe as well as comfortable. In time, you will know who you can and cannot trust as a friend. Letting go is the first step to the new you.

CHAPTER SEVEN
LIES YOU TELL YOURSELF

When are you going to stop lying to yourself about what happened that awful night you were spending time with one of your "best friends"? Or at least, that is what you tell yourself. Why can't you face what has happened to you? No, you were not in jail or the prison system when you were attacked and raped by another man; someone you trusted and thought was your friend. What do you remember about the rape? Were you forced down or tied up? Did you see this coming? The truth is when someone is attacked, they are caught off-guard and wonder what they did to trigger such behavior.

Below is a list of lies you tell yourself in order to feel as if you had some form of control over what took place.

- I think I wanted it.

- I allowed it to happen and knew what I was doing.

- No one took advantage of me, I let them.

- I went back a few times to show that I had control over this.

The truth is if another man makes a sexual comment at you, whether you thought something or not, only to end up being raped later or feeling as if you were talked into having sex, or worst, taken advantage of when you were drunk, you were a victim of rape. Stop making excuses for your attacker no matter how close they are to you and may have wanted it.

Were you told by another man what he wanted to do to you? Did you say anything? Were you afraid? Did you just accept what was told to you? Rape is rape no matter how you look at it, whether you said no or not. If someone takes the relationship to another level and expects you to do what they tell you; it is rape. Stop lying to yourself; it is not going to change what has happened. By lying to yourself, you are in a constant loop of thinking you deserved this type of treatment by a male counterpart. So you allowed yourself to be used and abused all because you have told yourself that it was okay or worst, you wanted it too. You tell yourself all these in a bid to hide the shame of feeling helpless in the presence of other men.

Did you know that when you allow other men to do what they want to you; you are allowing yourself to live in your victim stage? This does not mean you are at fault for what has happened to you, not at all. But it does shine the light on why you are allowing yourself to become a victim; be it in your mind or by what other men do to you when no one is around. If this is what you want; to sleep with other men, why are you not out looking for them on your own? Why do your sexual encounters with other men only take place after alcohol as if you can't face yourself afterwards? Stop lying and confusing yourself. As you can tell, working around in a state of sexual confusion is not fun nor is it if you are not gay, but act so because of your experiences, rapes!

For many men who battle sexual confusion after rape, they live double lives. While one says they are men, the other says they are looking for an encounter. So they think and begin to want something that has hurt them, confused them and left them in shame. This may mean your friendships are limited because you are not capable of having healthy relationships with other men due to the experiences of manipulation, helplessness as well as the loss of control. This can result in you seeing yourself not as an equal but a victim.

The more you read the more you will see that you are not gay because you were raped. Were you confused after the rape? Were you still talking to the person who had taken advantage of you days, weeks, months or even years later? Did you find it hard to cut ties with your rapist? Did you know that many victims of rape go through these same mixed and confusing emotions especially when they know the person that attacked them?

Know that not all rapes will be brutal or even aggressive. Some in fact are done where you end up feeling as if you were a willing participant. As you can see, women go through the same thing and some women stay with their attacker where they are constantly victimized. Many men have expressed to feeling humiliated by their attacker leading up to the rape.

Do you see that this was not your doing but the doing of the rapist. In order to get you in a weakened state, some even make fun of your size as well as your height. What may seem like innocent play at first, leaves you feeling humiliated and have a feeling of not being able to protect yourself, in the end.

I say you are not gay because someone who is gay and knows it is not being talked into it or used because they are afraid to fight back and find themselves giving in as their way of gaining some control over an already messed up situation. Don't allow rape to steal your mind by leaving you forever in a state of mistrust, confusion and fear. Your voice has been altered, if not stripped away but know that your voice is there and does not have to exist as a victim of rape.

Give yourself something you have not given it in a long time. That is the truth and how what has happened to you changed who you are. Know that you are strong and although you were a victim of rape, you are not a victim because you choose to not be and will no longer live in the shadows of fear and depression ever again.

You may have thought that you were safe because you were around a group of men when in fact you were not safe at all, and someone in the group hurt you. You trusted them and or knew them, be it well or not well enough when they raped you. What was clear is that they set their sights on violating you and nothing else. Now, you have found yourself in a place you never thought you would end up, being raped. I have spoken with men who were raped and won't say it was so but carry around a large amount of energy fueled by rage.

Were you raped as a child or teenager? Did this happen to you just as you were becoming a young adult and now your feelings about what you want is no longer clear because of what you experienced? You are a man and nothing or no one can take that away from you. Below is a list of things you need to do in order to get yourself past the denial stage:

- I was raped, and it happened to me when I was ……. (fill in the blank since you have the timeline.)

- I no longer need to hide from the truth.

- Being raped by another man was awful but it had nothing to do with my sexual orientation.

- Knowing who I am is important to my recovery and healing.

- Being raped by a man does not make me gay.

- Rape has nothing to do with race, one's sexual origin, economic status, religion or culture. It is all about control and fear.

- Telling the truth is the only way I can truly heal.

It is okay to be sad and angry from time to time but the key is to not let what has happened to you consume your life to where you are not able to live or see past the rape. Life is on the other side of any traumatic event!

CHAPTER EIGHT
SEXUAL CONFUSION

By now we all know that rape destroys the lives of its victims leaving them haunted, depressed and confused about their sexual orientation which takes a toll on everyone involved in that person's life. I no longer want to keep using the word *victim* since we all have the power and control to change how we see ourselves; so I will say *overcomer*.

Even if you don't see yourself at this moment as an overcomer; know that you are. Your life, I am sure, has taken you through ups and downs and you may have even seen things that left you wondering what just happened. You are not alone in the way you are feeling.

Did you know that one of many feelings a man can have after being raped by another man is sexual confusion? Did you know that many men who are raped as men can look back in life and find where they were molested by some close relative or family friend? Your pain and hurt is probably the only thing you can think about right now. That is okay since the healing stages for what you are going through will take you into many dark places mentally and emotionally before you get your healing.

Most men who were raped try to carry on in life as if nothing ever happened to them, only to hit a brick wall later on. Upon hitting this brick wall, I have spoken to a few friends of mine who experienced such horrific events that left them not being able to function in their day-to-day life or be around others. Many, who were outgoing and fun to be around, in turn imprison their emotions and heart because they are not able to look at themselves in the mirror.

Those who experience sexual confusion after being raped by another man find themselves crippled in everything they know to be true. Normal interactions with loved ones or spouses end up being an everyday struggle. Not only does the person who was raped suffer but their loved ones also, because such persons have lost the ability to show love or be happy when around their loved ones.

Below is a list of signs that show you are affecting those around you:

o   You lash out at anyone who seeks after your time or closeness.

o   You are afraid to show love or concern.

o   You question the motives of those around you and find trusting to be a major part of your ability to heal.

o   You ask or don't ask questions and go along with the plan only because you are afraid to show your feelings or say what is on your mind.

o   You disconnect with those around you and find it hard to build new relationships.

o   You are always unsure of your surroundings.

o   You feel like everyone is judging you.

o   You feel as if others in your family are laughing at you.

- You no longer trust being in the company of men alone.

- You are constantly seeking validation from men.

- You find it hard to enjoy life or your family, and bonding time with anyone becomes a battle.

Is there a way to stop feeling as if you are not the man your family or spouse sees you as? Yes, you can stop those feelings. But first, you have to look deep within yourself and assure yourself that you are safe. You also have to stop blaming yourself for the past and see that life has given you the ability to start anew. The more you work on you and allow your loved ones to assist; the more you will be in control.

Once you know that the power you need is within you, this is when you will see clearly who and what you are. When something happens to you that you can't explain, the mind tries to reason with it or understand what has happened to you. I can tell you that many of my friends who are dealing with this today are going through just that.

They are lost and at times confused about even being in their relationship. Everything seems to rub them the wrong way and they struggle with peace of mind. How many times do you catch your loved one trying to make sense of what has happened to them? Do you make them feel worse by the way you look at them? Do you question their sexuality at times? It is not enough to question your own sexuality after rape but to have others question you as a rape victim; it is heartbreaking!

How can they find some sense of closure to a horrible act? The only way to find your way back to the place you were before you were ever attacked is through accepting yourself as you are today.

If you are feeling as if nothing around you is making sense, you are on your way to healing and as you have guessed it is not going to be an easy road since the thing that is blocking your ability to move forward or even let go, is your mind. It is in your mind that you have flashbacks of the rape no matter how long ago it was. It is also in your mind where many of your thoughts and beliefs were stripped away when you got raped. No, you did not go to jail nor did you encounter this experience by a stranger. No, it was someone you looked up to, trusted, cared about and even believed in.

What if I told you that this person had the problem stuck in their minds and not you, I am sure you would agree but that is not all. You are agreeing to the fact that the process of establishing relationships was also made confusing after the rape. Below are ways you can help yourself get past your hurt and start enjoying your family and life again:

o   When negative thoughts creep up in your head to put you down, you tell yourself that it is not your fault and you are a man, husband, son, brother or father.

o   Give yourself credit for keeping it together when times were hard or building new relationships when you were afraid to.

o   Forgive yourself for hating and hurting yourself and those around you after the rape.

o   Get rid of people who mean you no good but seek to make you feel or look bad.

o   Trust your instinct when it tells you something is wrong or when making new friendships or building on old relationships. There is a reason you are not happy about this person in your life. Make the connection to whatever it is that is making you uncomfortable, and move on.

o   Take your time when it comes to letting go and know that you will not feel this way forever even if that is how you have been feeling for the past years.

Just because you are struggling with your sexual identity doesn't mean that you have to run around town sleeping with every woman you see. If you are thinking this is going to help you feel like a man, it won't. It will only make you feel worse when it is over because of the reason why you are doing it. Using other people to make you feel as if you matter is not taking control but rather giving up whatever control you have left.

If you can change anything about your feelings, what would they be? I like to ask this question no matter what the situation is because it shows you just how much control you have. Knowing that you can change or make changes to better yourself is all about control. If you were to say you could change how you feel from day to day, the next question would be; how can you make that happen? Why aren't you doing that now? We all have the power and ability to change our situation if we take it but many times, the blindness of reliving what has happened to you gets in the way. At that stage, you are tuned into your flashbacks of the past like watching a television show. It is your job to interrupt those flashbacks when they flood your head and views.

It is your job to speak life in the place of death even if that death is now being relived only in your mind. Your current state of confusion about what you are sexually attracted to is based on you beliefs and views.

Have your beliefs or views changed since the rape? Now ask yourself, where did it go? Can you look deep within yourself and see that they have been pushed aside but still with you? Nonetheless, it is your responsibility to go in and retrieve all of those things deep within you that you thought you have lost due to the selfish act. You also need to realize you are in control of your healing, going forward.

Know that not everyone is going to be in your corner and want you to heal. Doesn't that sound crazy and sick? You have to want more than anything to heal and not care about what people think of you. Caring about how people see you can make you an enemy of your own mind; one thing you must avoid. I see this happen time and time again, the person is lost afterwards. If you never had to fight for anything in your life, this is your fight. Getting back to the person you were before the attack is where you are trying to get to, if not becoming better than you were before the attack.

Change can only take place if you allow it to, and will never force you to do anything. You are the only one in control of letting change happen, so what are you waiting for? I want you to see yourself like you never saw yourself before as a winner. The more you see yourself in this way, the stronger you will become and that is the road you are walking on now. Know that you are not alone and every day somewhere, a young man is attacked. He never saw it coming just like you and like you, he will have to pull himself up out of that hole.

It will take everything inside of you. You will need to use some parts of your body for support more than other parts to get yourself to where you need to be. But it is worth it and you are the only one that can do it, no matter how hard and frightening it seems. You will depend on your arms and hands in the beginning stages of pulling yourself up out of that deep dark place. So look around for something you can grip onto. No matter how small or narrow that place is that you are gripping to pull yourself up, do so and hold fast onto it. Next, your feet need to position you for any future jumps ahead and your knees need to be ready to help you crawl upwards if you have to. Now see your hands, arms and feet as your mind, body and soul! When you work with every part of you as a whole; you teach your mind how to live and let go!

CHAPTER NINE
LETTING GO OF THE PAST

Not everyone is ready to let go of a beautiful memory. So they visit that memory from time to time which leaves them with that old feeling of the experience whenever they want it. How many times have you thought about something; be it negative or positive that was just a glimpse of an event from your past? How often do you see those images in your head? Did you know that getting out of the past has more to do with your thinking than anything else? It is true you are long gone since those events took place, yet when you think about them; you are filled with warm or hurtful feelings.

When you train your way of processing and storing information from your past, you allow yourself to stay hurt, fearful and sometimes broken. It is not fun when your mind won't let go of a traumatizing event and keeps you viewing as if you enjoy it.

Learning to let go is just one of the many things you will learn in this chapter since we all relived something from day to day whether we want to or not.

Your fear and trauma connect with your mind and cause your mind to lose control over the ability that gives you the control over many of your experiences. So as you can see, not all memories are pleasant. For victims of rape or sexual assault, the automatic button is stuck on playback in that individual's head with no way of turning it off or stopping it. This is freighting for anyone who has been a victim. You must learn to change the channel, as one would say, in your head in order to control what you want to relive which is for some not always easy to do. If you have ever been a victim, you will know what it is that I am talking about.

How do you make it stop? How many times have you heard someone say that to you because their minds won't let go of the past. It keeps them in a prison of events no one would dream of reliving. Too many times when someone is trying to get over something, they struggle with the past even if the past is not in their way, their mind pulls that information up for them to relive as if it was yesterday.

Understanding why your mind remembers certain things is crucial to where in your mind that information is stored. It is more than you in that your mind is not letting go now. How about your heart and emotions? Yes, they too are tied into what your mind wants you to relive.

It is your mind that still to this day thinks it is a victim even when it happened years ago. I discovered while talking with friends of mine who were raped that their biggest setbacks were not starting over. Their biggest setbacks are their minds, telling them that they can't move on because they are still afraid, hurt, angry, depressed, tired and suicidal, through its constant programming of flashback images of rape or sexual assault. Why can't I just forget what happened to me and live my life? Is it always pressing on the mind of a victim of rape? If you pay attention, your mind thinks that it is helping you to let go when in fact it is doing the complete opposite!

Did you know that when you don't give the mind what it is looking for, it keeps you in a constant loop of flashbacks as if you will know how to help it? These flashbacks can be during the day, at night while you are sleeping or during any time of the day. The key to letting go of your pain and hurt is by telling your mind and heart it is no longer going through that event and that in fact, you are no longer in danger as it is having you to feel or believe.

When you are in this stage or training your mind to let go more times than you will want to encounter, it will always take place with an array of emotions that somewhat throws you back at the exact day and time things happened. If you can remember while this is happening, tell yourself this is true and my mind won't let go because it is sick and saddened over the last strong emotion that I had no matter if it is bad or good. Your mind must take responsibility for keeping you in the past or it will make you blame everything and everyone around you.

Your mind is not trying to hurt you but holding on to strong connections and emotions through your experiences if that makes any sense to you. When your mind feels that it no longer needs those events or emotions, it will let them go but you can help it to do so sooner than later. Below are lists of command words you can program your mind to know when you feel the need to snap out of a bad experience due to a flashback:

Wait a minute, this command you say to your mind in the middle of a flashback puts those images on pause while you gather yourself and take control of your reality.

- o Summer days: this is a command that you say to your mind that can instantly change what you are reliving while giving you control to relive a more pleasant memory.

- o Hot Tub: this is a command that you say to your mind to get it back to a place you enjoyed. This command can be beach, pool and Jacuzzi. Once you get the picture, and so will your mind.

- o If I say I love you: it is a command that you say to your mind when you want it to relive an old flame or first love. I am sure you can experience pleasant thoughts here.

o   Cheese, depending on the smell, is a command that you say to your mind to have it stop flashing you in its tracks and sends a message to your stomach instead of your mind.

If you ask me how this can help you to forget, I will tell you easy. You have done this a thousand times without knowing it naturally. No matter if it was a thought, word phrase or command word you used, it stopped you from thinking about what happened to you and refocused your mind on something completely different.

This is the same way you can be fussing about something and someone or something interrupts you, changing the focus in the room and the energy. You stop arguing and all parties focus on the thing or person that changes the subject without them knowing. You can learn more about reprogramming one's self in my upcoming book, *Heart Bruised Conscious Connection*. For now, I want you to learn how to give your mind and emotions simple and easy to remember commands.

Can giving yourself commands to help you stop focusing on a rape really help you in letting go? The answer is yes. But it is how much you want it that makes the difference. If you tell yourself that this is the only way you can get over your rape and stop having those flashbacks, then you are on your way to healing. This is more than just the power of words. Yes words are included in the process but it is how you use those words to change the channel in your mind that brings about the needed result.

Picture yourself when you think about something that makes you upset and use a command word that you feel connected to because it is connected to an event you relive every time you mention that word. That is how it works! I have told many of my friends that the best way to train their minds on how to change the channel to something that makes them feel good is to practice this technique with everyday thoughts. The key is to see how many times you can change your thoughts to something else while in the middle of another thought. Simple enough, right?

Just like the breathing you do every day already, without planning or thinking to do so beforehand. This is how commanding your mind with words works. The problem is when those thoughts become dark and depressing, your inner workings are caught off-guard and you find yourself forced to watch those images in your head because you are not thinking or knowing how to stop them. It is as if your mind wants you to relive every shocking moment.

When you see letting go in this format, you soon realize that it is not the event you are trying to relive but rather, the flashbacks of those moments which you now have control over.

When you learn the proper method of letting go, you learn how to leave many negative and painful events unwatched by a simple command which pretty soon your mind won't even challenge you into watching because it knows the command word you use to stop it so well. Now are you ready to let go? Have you thought of that special command you want to use to snap your mind out of flashing you with negative and horrific past events? You are the MASTER of your own mind and what you choose to relive. Don't ever think that you are stuck with the images in your head, you are NOT.

Don't ever think you are forced to have to relive a rape or sexual assault, you don't. Your mind knows that you can control what you want to think about or not think about by placing events, symbols or commands in your head that link it back to an event you don't mind reliving. Now that you know how to let go, don't let anything stop you ever again!

Now that you see yourself letting go, how does it feel? Do you still have much of the anger? Know that from time to time, you will still feel much of those emotions. Don't be discouraged; what you feel is the leftover residue from the event, and in time you will not feel those emotions. Like with anything, once you have made up your mind to stop hurting, you stop hurting. Simple as that.

I guess it is true that when you are tired of something, you have no reason to hold on to it and find letting go of it to be easy. Your mind and heart has a way of holding on to things it deems important even if those things affect and impact you in a negative way. When you find yourself fighting to hold on to the past, don't! Learn how to invest your time and energy into healing every part of you, not just when you are feeling down and depressed.

If you have picked up an addiction as a way to cope, now is the time to let that go as well; whatever it is. You don't need to drown your sorrows or take your mind off thinking about the past through drugs or alcohol; you just need to face yourself in the mirror. Since being raped, you have picked up on a lot of nasty behaviors. You know for sure that is not you or who you are. I am sure being under the influence of something may feel good in covering up your pain but you notice how fast those feelings and emotions come rushing back to you when you are no longer high or wasted? So using something to help you let go is not really letting go; it is called coping.

Stop drowning your sorrow and pain in pills, booze, women or drugs. Neither one of them can make you feel the way you want to feel. You are stronger than you know and now is the time that you become that person. If I can see you as an overcomer; you should be able to see yourself in that light!

CHAPTER TEN
I'M OKAY

You are okay. So you say while each day your world has been altered by your past. Allowing yourself to cry when you are sad or mad is human and helps to purge those bottled up emotions of energy you keep stored inside. What did your attacker leave you with besides hurt, shame and anger? How about this confused state of mind that you now carry around with you? Learn how to face your demons without the need to flee or else; you would only be brought back at a later date to face it.

I know you want this to pass by so that you can get back to living. You have not been alive since something was stolen from you that you want back. Yet, you tell yourself while turning up or shooting up, *I'm okay*. You are not okay and haven't been in a long time, in fact you hurt more now than you did the day you were raped.

You keep old friends around, including your rapist because you did have a good friendship before you were taken advantage of in your drunken state of mind. Did you tune out like so many victims of rape do or were you so full of alcohol that you couldn't care less? Why won't you admit that you are still hurting so that you can take control of what is real; your hurt and shame.

Keeping around people who were present in your life when you were raped can be a constant reminder of what happened to you especially when those so called friends are still connected directly or indirectly to the person that raped you. Now do you see that you are not okay? Now do you see that you are still affected by your past? The only thing that has moved on has been time, yet you are still trapped in between the past and present. If this is your truth and you feel that you can live with it, do so. But if you are looking to let go to be okay, you have to admit that you are not okay and work from there to where you want to be.

You are not a rape victim but a living and breathing wonderful human being. Hurts and pains do heal. See yourself in a new life and have fun. If this means you need to connect with people who understand you, do so. This does not mean you need validation from anyone especially another man. Below is a list of reasons why a rape victim may seek new relationships with other men.

o   Validation; you are looking for another man to give you back your manhood.

o   Approval; you are looking for the respect of another man to see you as his equal and not his prey!

It sounds silly when you really look at it, doesn't it? The truth is that many men who have been the victims of male on male rape seek those two as if their lives depend on it. They are looking to ways their manhood as well as their respect will be handed back to them. But if you must look for your manhood or if you have forgotten where to find it, simply look down and just under your belt you will find it! If that is not enough, look inside of yourself and the views and customs that the men of your family or someone taught you, they are still there as parts of you.

I know you might feel this is not enough nor does your penis define who and what you are. Then why is it now or why are you allowing someone else's penis to define you?

You know where your penis goes but the rapists did not. They took it upon themselves to use you for their gain but not only did they use you; they used themselves. The person that has done this to you must also be in pain. They pass on to you what they only knew of, assault. This is why you tell yourself you are okay; you are not in pain like the person who goes around raping other men. Doesn't it make you wonder what could have happened in their lives to keep them in so much turmoil? Your attacker has much more to face other than knowing how they are feeling from day to day. Just like you, they are questioning themselves and their behavior.

Why should you care what the rapist is going through is what you may be thinking. The answer is simple; because they cared about affecting and hurting you. They live in a world of seeking out validation and approval and because they have not gotten it, they take it out on others in order to feel in control while rewarding themselves through rape. Now ask yourself again if you are okay. If you can learn to be truthful with yourself, you have the mind of someone who is constantly seeking male validation and approval.

Does this mean you go out tomorrow and start trusting people? No. What it means is that you are no longer a victim. You are very much aware of who and what you are; a man who just had something horrible happen to him but it did not break him, although it could have. It did not kill him although it could have, and it did not change the makeup of his anatomy. When you look at things from these glasses, you see why you want to feel you are okay versus being okay.

No one said that life was fair or perfect. It is your job to take those imperfect times in life to use as fuel for gaining control over your life in order to make a change for others. Many men are standing where you are right now, including people you know who have yet to say they have been raped and are learning how to breathe and cope with the simple things in life. Many men look at other men, thinking that they have something other men don't have when in fact, that man or group of men you are looking up to may have been raped or be the one who committed the rape. Just like someone will never know you were raped; this is true for anyone because no one knows what a rape victim looks like.

Stop being jealous of men you think have not gone through anything, we all have gone through something in life. If you don't know anything, know that life teaches everyone hurt, pain, fear, depression, neglect, shame and guilt and it does not discriminate. In a sense, we all must learn how to be okay and mean it. We all must learn how to trust our feelings or change the images we see. This is not one man's battle but one the human race struggles with daily. Therefore, stop giving in to false feelings because in the end, you only play yourself.

Life as we know it has a crazy way of getting your attention in which we learn how our minds truly react to something that hurts us. You mind has a way of brushing everything off as if it is no big deal while keeping you locked inside as it seeks to understand all. Why do you say you are okay when clearly you are not? Saying you are okay to a few people around you is one thing but telling yourself that when you know it is not the truth is something completely different.

This alone should make you stand up and take notice to what is going on inside of you since you are not the only one dealing with being raped but your mind body and soul is. Boy it does have a way of getting your attention! When you find yourself just agreeing with your reasoning to understand or deal with yourself, emotions, feelings, anger, shame and guilt; that is when you tell yourself, I am not okay!

It is right standing up for the truth; your truth and stop painting a pretty picture to an ugly and nasty event. There is nothing wrong with saying you are not okay. When you do this, it forces your mind to make the corrections and not you. Below is a list of what happens when you stand up for yourself and not allow your mind to play games with you:

o   You become stronger.

o   You know what the truth is and don't need to cover it up.

o   You are facing your pain and demons head on.

o   You are living in the moment and nothing else.

o   You force your mind to make the correction and not tell you what you can and cannot feel.

o   You stop living in denial and fear.

o   You see yourself past the victim and survivor stage.

o   You are no longer afraid of the truth, your truth and who and what has happened to you.

o   Your mind processes your acceptance of denying it and knowing the truth as strength.

o   Your mind follows your lead.

o   Your mind stops trying to make sense of what happened to you and trust that you have processed everything and is ready to move on.

The choice to move forward and challenge yourself by not giving in to what your mind wants in order to gloss over things is your overcoming not just being raped and living as a survivor, but living as an overcomer.

CHAPTER ELEVEN
RECOVERY ZONE

You have gotten yourself together and as a survivor, you are still having a hard time dealing with the fact that you were a victim of rape. You are not sure where to turn for help and counseling in your community. No matter how much you tell yourself that you are just fine, you are not okay. You struggle with your bad days outnumbering your good days, then let me be the first to tell you that you need help in getting past what has happened to you.

You don't have to go through this alone. There are places and counseling that can help you deal with your emotions and feelings. You need to get out your anger and pain so that you can live a life with no flashbacks. I know you are still having flashbacks. They may not be as frequent but they are still there, locked away in the corners of your mind. I want to see you overcome this, not just survive it.

You are whatever you register yourself to be in your mind; you are no longer a victim! It is not your fault and you should know that. How long has it really been since you were able to laugh and have a good time? Is your mind still keeping you in the past with flashbacks of things you don't want to see? Do you feel like you have tried everything you could do and nothing worked because you are still waking up in the middle of the night in cold sweats with your heart pounding out of your chest? Is the rape a constant lingering thought that never leaves your mind no matter what you are doing? You have the power to stop everything that is going on inside of you right now because just like you want answers to what the heck happened to you; so does your mind, body and soul.

Stop living in the shadows of what was and come out in the open and live. Just when you think that you are past it, something triggers a horrible thought in your head, right? Many times, when we think we are doing our self a favor in not talking about the past, we only end up hurting more and that pain is deep. Below is a list of things you can do to help you move forward as an overcomer:

o   Take up a new sport or hobby.

o   Read books that inspire you to make changes in your thought process.

o   Do community work or rescue an animal in need of a home. You would be surprised how much having a pet can brighten your days and help to bring healing in your life.

o   Tell your story even if that means just writing it down but change the ending. See yourself making changes in how you want the ending to be.

Did you know that you have the power to rewrite your life? You don't have to be a writer to give yourself a new beginning. The longer you think about what has happened to you, the more you will find yourself in a dark place where getting out is almost impossible. Your mental breakthrough starts with you and you alone. No one can stop the flashbacks, but just you. No one can stop the pain, hurt and shame, but only you. I want you to stop hurting and beating yourself up over what you should and could have done to prevent being raped. Get the thought of what you could have done out of your head because it says you did not do enough and that is not true.

If you have stopped living and going out, I want you to get up and live. That does not mean you should put yourself in a position that makes you feel uncomfortable. Do things that once made you happy and feel good inside. Don't let your mind keep you from life and who you really are. More importantly is having a strong support system around you where you are reminded daily that it is not your fault and nothing is wrong with you.

Don't let what other people think of you be the reason you are not overcoming your past. There are a number of things those around you can do if they are not sure how to help you. Asking you if you are alright or how you are feeling throughout the day is not it; trust me. I know it sends a not so good feeling to you, right? Below is a list of what your loved ones can do to help you move past those moments when you find yourself mentally stuck and emotionally drained:

- Be understanding and treat you the same.

- Keep you laughing and smiling.

- Get you out of the need to be alone by getting you to do something fun.

- Listen to you if all you want to do is talk and never read anything into what you are saying.

- If you really need time to yourself, they should make sure that they are not far away and can be there for you when you are no longer feeling down.

- Let you know that they love you and care about your wellbeing.

- Tell you when you begin to place blame on yourself that it is not your fault.

- Shouldn't be angry if you are sad or lash out. They should understand that it is your way of purging. All they need do is to just back off and give you time.

o   Know that you will have a mixture of emotions and at times, it will seem as if you are cycling on a rollercoaster and they are strapped in the seat next to you; this is normal.

In the midst of those crazy moments you will feel less of yourself. As weird as it sounds, this crazy kind of normal is what I like to call things that we do when we have been influenced or altered in some way. For what you have gone through, it is okay. Making it back to yourself all in one piece is the only focus here and nothing else. Knowing this is why it is so crucial for you to have the right people in your corner as well as a part of your support group. As you grow and vent and go through the many stages of becoming more than just a survivor but an overcomer, you will learn that the journey was worth it, in the end! Now see yourself as I see you; an overcomer and live life because you deserve it!

CHAPTER TWELVE
LISTEN TO YOUR HEART

Not much is said about the heart when it comes to trauma. That is why I have decided to add this last chapter in. Did you know that whatever it is in life you face, those emotions and feelings must be dealt with just like anything and everything else? Don't think for one minute that you are going to get past all of this hurt and pain without confronting your heart. You are wrong! What does your heart have to do with the fact that you were raped and probably more than once? It has a lot to do with how you are feeling at this moment. The nights you lay awake in your bed crying has nothing to do with those feelings just jumping up on you. On the other hand, it has more to do with an angry and hurting heart, and both can keep you stuck and to not really get over anything. Your mind is not the only enemy you have to deal with and battle day to day, but the fact that you know or don't know the individual who raped you.

If you don't listen to anything else, I ask that you learn to listen to your heart. When it is in pain, it has its own way of keeping you safe. But you have to know when the pain is due to your past and not because you are emotional about some new events. Have you done everything you can to stop the pain in your heart? Trauma affects every aspect of your life; not just your mind and emotions but you as a whole. You may think that you need to face the person who hurt you, or go after them to find healing. Know that that is not always the case. Running around to get everyone's attention that has hurt you is not going to stop your heart and may only numb the pain you feel day to day for a short time. I promise you that you will be disappointed when you discover the hurt and pain you thought you can get rid of is not leaving and despite all the efforts and attempts outside of yourself to get the healing that you need, nothings working. If this is the case right now; it is because your heart needs your attention and not the attention influenced by revenge and anger. You must let your heart know that in your efforts to trust, you were hurt and that the hurt hunts you at times which leaves you living as a shall of yourself.

Below is a list of things you can do to gain back the trust of your heart that you will keep yourself safe as well as heed any warnings you feel from within; many would call it intuition.

o   Acknowledge you have been hurt.

o   Be patience knowing that your healing is taking place every day even if you don't feel it.

o   Learn to listen to your intuition; it will never leave you astray and is here to guide you.

o   Know that it was not your fault, plain and simple.

o   Stop worrying about what others are saying about you; their opinion does not make or break you.

o   Change your way of thinking and how you see the world around you. The more you are aware; the better off you will be inside.

- It is never too late to tell someone you know and love. Trust that everyone is not looking at you as if it is your fault.

- Face your fears, shame and anger head on so that you are not acting out these feelings and emotion in your daily life. It can cost you much more than you are ready to give up.

- Stand up for what is right and never drop your head. Yes what happened to you was not right but you should not be the one living your life in a dark corner.

The more you see yourself and your heart in a healing state; the more you will start to see yourself in that place. Know that you will never get the answer to the question many raped victims ask. Why? No one is going to give you the answer you need to put your life back together; you have to do that yourself. Although it is unfair, you are not alone since many people; male and female are on the same road as you. If you can dream it, your can have peace of mind and anything else that you want.

Know that at times, you will not feel safe with your loved ones or friends, and that is okay. You have nothing to prove to anyone. Your proof is only to yourself and it should be that you are getting stronger and overcoming what has happened to you daily whether you feel, see it or believe it. Positive thought is the lifeline to your true healing and know that you will have many more bad days before good ones. You are getting past it and that is all that matters.

Below is a list of things that can keep you from growing and overcoming you pain/hurt:

o   Stressing out over what happened to you can keep you feeling depressed.

o   Lying to yourself about what really happened to you and who is at fault.

o   Self-blame is easy since you have to face yourself in the mirror.

o   Unwilling to forgive yourself and the person who have done this to you.

The more you lie to yourself about growth or feeling sad, the more likely you find it hard to let go and get past those things that hunt you. When you come to grips with your life, face to face with your hurt and pain; then and only then can you identify the root cause of your hurt. Perhaps, you have forgiven the person who has done this to you but just not yourself, because somewhere in the back of your mind, you hold yourself responsible for everything even though common sense tells you it is not your fault.

If you are not finding the help you need, please refer back to chapter eleven for resources that can help you find and accept the person inside of you that is in search of love and respect that is within us all.

Printed in Great Britain
by Amazon